Espresso Boy

Coby Jones

Presentation by *BookLeaf Publishing*

Web: www.bookleafpub.com

E-mail: info@bookleafpub.com

ISBN: 9789363305045

First edition 2024

ACKNOWLEDGEMENT

I know it's cliche and everything, but there are a couple of people that I would like to thank for forming who I am as a writer.

Thank you to the literary greats that got me interested in books: Mary Shelley, Edgar Allen Poe, Franz Kafka, Fyodor Dostoevsky, Herman Melville, Byung-Chul Han, and Sarah Kane.

An even greater thank you to Harry Baker and George Watsky, for getting me into poetry.

And, somehow, an even greater than the, above, even greater thank you to Marshall Mathers (Eminem).

Finally, I would like to thank my (not quite, but basically) editor; Viya.

PREFACE

This is my first book to have published, and while the writing of this poetry collection has been nothing short of a wild ride, I am very proud of how the collection has come together to tell the most authentically me story. Or, as my unpaid "editor", Viya, put it "The most Coby Jones series of words that have ever been written next to each other".

In my debut poetry collection I really tried to tell my own story. I tried as hard as I could to put the most vulnerable parts of myself into poetry. All before turning to our ridiculous world and pointing out the worst parts of our current society in the most satirical manner I can manage. Highlighting my deep beliefs in Feminism and Mental Health.

And finally, I left a lot of hidden easter eggs in these poems. Little ways that they connect whether with similar rhyme schemes, obvious word repetitions, or intentional miscapitalizations. Though I feel I must warn the reader that I have been heavily influenced by contemporary poets and post-modernist writers, and so my writing might occasionally come across as slightly abstract. I assure you, it is intentional.

My deepest and most sincere hope for the readers of this collection is that they find at least one poem that really touches them. Something that they can truly connect with. I hope I can make every reader laugh at least once, and maybe even tear up at least once.

I do really hope that you enjoy all of these poems, and have an absolutely spectacular day!

Uninspired Poetry

Uninspired poetry,
It's just stuff that I scribble when I feel like I'm
not quite alive.
It's the words inscribed on sides of my mind
from
Funerals, and fights, and having to watch people
who can't see they're beautiful.
So while a few of my poems may be clever and
full of fun little rhymes,
Poetry is just how I cope with my issues.

But, of course, my poetry has to be different.
And not just 'cause I'm an addict for being a
tack in the backside of normalcy.
Normally, it's 'cause the girls I've asked out
actually act smacked,
They're taken aback, shocked,
Go anaphylactic from stacks of lactic acid
I packed with yaks and yapping.
It's practically disastrous
This back-tickling madness.
Thus you can imagine I don't write much
romantic stuff.
Plus, I tend to use poetry to choke-to-ease the
things I think

About overused trends, abuse, and global
decrees in the world.
Then, unfurling in pursuing my own emotions,
I'll advertise my own adversity in verse.
Inverse all the sin, hurt, and Jinns cursed to
haunt me.
Lips pursed, and tricks furnished, I'll flip, turn,
what the world taught me
To finish my thirty third variation on
commentary of nation,
Question the placement of already breaking
social stations,
And the phasingly misplaced facade-based
phases of "this is pace" people pushing hatred.
It's just the way that these phrases create my
disdain
As I'm gravely losing my patience with doctors
screwing their patients.
'Cause it just feels like everyone takes
Anything and everything that they can in any
situation.
…
I can slip into free verse
And talk about myself.
Talk about my "overbearing sixteen year old
trauma".
Use my metaphors to
Go deeper than the deepest metaphors on the
poet-tree.

Because in the end aren't all poets
A branch off the same tree
Of human emotions?
Before I go post-modern on you and repeat
Repeat repeat repeat repeat repeat repeat repeat
repeat repeat repeat repeat repeat repeat repeat
repeat repeat repeat repeat repeat repeat repeat
repeat repeat repeat repeat repeat repeat repeat
repeat repeat repeat repeat repeat repeat repeat
repeat repeat repeat repeat repeat repeat repeat
repeat repeat repeat repeat repeat repeat repeat
repeat repeat repeat Repeat myself to prove a
point about abstract symbolism.
I'll signal "this is me" in poetry fueled by shots
of espresso.
Expressing myself tapping my foot to "off the
rack" rap tracks.
Popping a handful of M&M's bobbing my head
to Eminem,
Hoppin' in my seat to Hopsin, and falling off it
with Watsky,
Sinking into my peak inspired arch as I hark the
screams from Linkin Park.
Because this music puts me in NF-ing ninth
cloud
Where I can write, and be proud that my mind is
so loud.
And even when it gets to be loud enough to
pounce on my mental health;

I just count through A,B,C,D12 times.
Then go guzzle more of Harry Baker's dozens of
poems,
Get some of Andrea Gibson,
Throw a fit as I cry through Kafka 'cause I know
it hurts.
And somewhere, in those other artists words,
I find my uninspired poetry.

Quantum Physics

What if everyday things could be turned into poetry?
Like, if a bug sting was a poem, would it bee bad?
Or maybe it would cause a lot of buzz and turn into a fad.
If chemistry was a poem… would it be impossible to pass?
That was a joke, I passed chemistry.
I mean, barely, but as long as we get the bare minimum
That's all it takes not to get blasted by your teacher.

What if Quantum Physics was a poem?
I don't think that anyone would understand it.
Because I think that every stanza it would change.
And anyone who reads it would read something different
Yeah, if Quantum Physics was a poem it would be a love poem.
Gross.

A Single People Poem

Why are the most romantic people always
single?
Like we just love so much that people can't take
it
And we can't seem to fake it enough to make it
seem normal.
So instead we take our heart out and offer it to
anyone who promises to break it
So badly we can tell ourselves we don't want to
feel again.
Then we'll fix it!
By being a fixture
Somewhere in between absolutely confident and
totally insecure.
A mixture of purely unsure, and astoundingly
certain
That it will all work out in the end.
But here we are,
Endlessly loving nothing.

We stare at rom-coms, slightly disgusted
'Cause we've discussed it, and we'd prefer more
of a horror movie.

Screw the "rom-communism" Stallin' 'till
you're boxed in prisms where you can't shine"
kind of love
See, I'd rather you give me the Bonnie and
Clyde, why not be willing to die, kind of girl by
my side.
The "spend half of our lives living with things
we aren't supposed to survive"
And the "stare down the Bears that're supposed
to scare us" kind of love.
I want the Mary Shelley kind of love.
Where when you're married she'll carry around
your heart once you die.
The Sarah Kane kind of
"Torture me until my veins bleed your name"
kind of love.
The Kafka kind of let us cry together and love
ourselves for our pain kind of love.
The "show me the darkest side of yourself and
I'll show you how much I love staring at stars in
the dark" kind of love.
The "I'm fine if I go totally stark because I
know you're the one I'll see in my hallucinatory
dreams" kind of love.
The kind of love that kills parts of you.
The kind of love that chases you with a knife
and makes you face your demons.
But people are scared of our kind of love
Because it's uncomfortable

And it's terrifying.
And people would rather live their dry lives
Than cry trying to die flying
High on the skies of real romance.

Language Barrier

In English we say words
Clever words, of course.
We use these arrangements of squiggly lines
To translate our surroundings into a language.

But in poetry we say…
Nothing

Because In poetry we just stare at empty pages
Trying to figure out how to translate our tears
into a language others can understand.
But that's just it, right?
Poets are so stuck on one side of a language
barrier that we can't express ourselves outside of
lines of rhymes.
We're so stuck loving things, that we can't ever
say it.
So caught screaming that we end up silent.
So caught becoming something that we lose
everything we tried to be.

In English we say "I hurt myself"
But in Poetry, we take our knives
And carve the pain into a page
Writing broken lines with our own blood.

In English we can say "I Love You"
But in poetry we infuse the idea of "you" into
our hearts
So when, in English, you say "I don't love you
anymore"
Poetry says…
Nothing
Because we can not comprehend a reality in
which you are not still our world.
In poetry we never stop loving
And no matter how many times we break our
own hearts
And rip the pages of our poems, trying to tear
ourselves apart
If a poet ever loves you…
They can't stop.

In English we say "we were never meant to be"
But in poetry…
In poetry we say:
I'm sorry.
I'm sorry that we couldn't be what we wanted to
be.
I am so sorry that I couldn't get over my
language barrier.

But English never responded to poetry
And she never responded to me.

If I Would Write a Love Poem

If...
If I would write a love poem...
It would suck.
Because I don't honestly want to think I've ever
really been in love.
I've had the blurry vision, heart palpitations, and
the staying up 'till 4 in the morning cause neither
of you could leave the conversation situations
but I've never had love.
So if I was to write a love poem, it would be sort
of an empty thing.
Like every stanza was cobweb short of an
abandoned house horror scene.
And anybody who's ever truly been in love
walking through the chambers of my heart
destined only for pumping blood through my
arts would drop to the floor and scream.
These metaphors they seem almost as if the
fourth wall, at its core was a screen
And behind it, an audience who wrote notes to
every rom com scene.
With dream boats floating in waterless streams.
Running from the horror movie monsters,

Hearts beating as they're chased by a blood
sucking vampire of love that can't be seen,
So he's forced to be that horrifying monster in
his own story.
If I was to write a love poem, it would be sad.
Because that's the only kind of relationship I've
ever had.
If I was to write a love poem it would start with
the lines "I am not enough"
And end with a clever way to say that pain is
love.
If I was to write a love poem it would start out
perfectly
Every perfect word and perfect beat in perfect
sync.
And when I would write this love poem
I would be shaking to the teeth
Wondering "does she even remember me?"
If I would write a love poem
It would be so bad that people might read it.
If I were to write a love poem I would begin
with the purpose of love and then defeat it,
Because the problem with putting love in a
poem when you've never felt the emotion by
itself is that everything you say is all too true.
The problem is that every line in your poem
writes you.
And it hurts.
So why don't I write this love poem?...

Fear.
Because if my heart's every failures have made
anything clear
It's that, first,
I need to learn to love the man in the mirror.

Love in a Toaster

Toast people…
Yes, those people
Who coast through their lives
With nothing but boring and dry
Toast.
They aren't on a kosher-light diet,
No one is toast-torturing them,
And they aren't forced to stay quiet.
They genuinely just chose to eat toast.
Gross.

The toast people who wake up every morning,
Groaning and moaning as they're throwing their
sheets over
And go about towing themselves towards their
kitchen.
Hitching themselves beside a fixture on the
counter, snug
And pitching a pitcher of pitch black coffee into
a mug.
Broadening their arms past a couple of cups in
the cupboard and nabbing the bread,
Then they shrug as they stick to fixing
themselves a dry piece of toast
With no fixin's or flavors from the table.

'Cause they try to keep it all stable.
They aren't able to think they're capable
Enough to make a full piece of bread
That isn't burnt worse than a record label
Recorded as saying cruel disses to Eminem and
his little misses.
And this is how the toast people eat their
breakfast, before
Dawning an unadored suit that doesn't fit and
they've never worn
Outside the wartorn boredom of toast office lore.
They're then caught in
Belittling their wife who hasn't been
kissed on the lips since…
At least a week or more.
And to top it all off they take a taxi, mentally
maxing in the back seat
So they don't walk on their feet past all the
wall's on the back street.
As his life becomes another Wall Street Story.
They slave away at that job that they hate,
And come back home to a wife they stopped
loving eight years ago.
The wife watches Her Man, "Mel" go Vile to the
core.
Ate dinner and had a fight
With kids they contemplated not having.
That night, they drank wine alone in a living
room

Where they've been stuck living since their
honeymoon,
But they can't afford to move
Because the job they so hate doesn't pay nearly
enough.
And it seems tough, this unbuffed life they run
through
But they can't feel anything after the
over-roasted
Toast life makes them make themselves
bulletproof.

Toast people, you'll later host remorse
Once you're…
Forced through a metamorphosis following
fortune to
Become A Responsible Type of Loser who Eeks
By. You
Become a bug on the wall, and crawl until
you're all but lost
You're getting burnt out, roasting at a high heat
on a
Burning-me burnt out society
Trying to churn out the driest type people.
Pushing themselves to be creatures
Featured on wrinkles in white T-shirts.
'Cause they're bleached
'Till their personality's burnt away.
And their freedom of speech turns

To say how tired they are
Of life being a leach-learning
To eat every part of the parts of themselves
That they're praying can stay.
Yeah, they're praying in preach-pews
For maybe a meet-cute
And maybe they meet a new someone who
Makes them feel like they aren't so beat.
But as life goes on your love's another wall on
the street
'Cause society says to buy a Ford
You buy it all, 'til you can't afford to be for love,
'Cause you're always on call
It's the cause in all ways of your fall,
Of your burnt out bad brain.
The reason no love is the same
After it's been burnt in the toaster where
everyone gains
Their money, their pride, and their reason for
dying.
"Don't you mean: reason for living?"
No, I mean: reason I'm writing this poem:
Because I watch these people as their love life
Flickers, it falters through all the tension, it
brittles
And breaks like the bread in the toaster it flakes
off,
'Till we all try to salvage what little is left.

These over-roasted "work to boost your boasted
boats 'till you're dead"
Toaster type person then tries to put their burnt
lives back in the toaster hoping to get bread.
But instead
They see what it's like to be one of the hundreds
Who never rose above losing their lust for
love…
In a toaster.

Life and Death

I like to imagine life as a beautiful woman.
She dances, and she sings.
Life is always smiling, and she's bubbly, and
sometimes she feels lonely
But she always looks happy.
Life believes in her God, and loves him from the
depths of her beating heart.

And I like to see death as a tortured man.
There is something chilling about death.
He has a hood over his face, so you can't tell if
he's really smiling.
But death is always at peace.
And Death doesn't believe in God,
Because he'd met God long ago.

One day,
Knowing they could never be together,
Life fell in love with death.
Staring into his eyes,
Life saw everything in Death's hidden soul.
But death refused to "love" Life back.

As the two slowly wove their souls together,
Death saw the pain growing inside of Life.

Death watched as Life pushed herself to look
even brighter,
Even happier,
Even more alive.
Life loved Death a little more every day,
But Death still never let his haunted house of a
heart say it loved anything.

Soon,
Death finally fell in love with life.
He never said it, but that day, when,
He looked deeply into her bright eyes,
Death saw everything.
Death saw the blood of injuries
And the tears of loss.
The blood empty love,
And pointless lives.
Death saw war,
And poverty,
And pain.
He saw the trillions of living things
So convinced that they were alive
They found it necessary to kill.
Death saw Life for how she tried to destroy
herself from the inside,
And Death saw the eternal suffering of living.
Death finally understood why Life had loved
Death,
Because Death may have been terrifying

But he was peace.
Death relieved those suffering from their pain.

When Death offered to help take away some of
her hurting
She said her God could do it.
But when Life ran to find God,
She stumbled into a dark abyss.
Confused and enraged,
Life killed herself,
But refused to let Death take her away.
Instead, choosing to exist like her creations, in a
dead body.
While Death had to keep moving on,
Bringing life to those his love could no longer
help.
And from that day,
Death went through every moment with Life in
his haunted heart.

Afraid

I used to be afraid of the dark
When my parents turned the lights off
The shadows from the sides of my room took the
chance to pounce
After I pranced into my room, no ounce of fear,
until it got dark in here
Because to the young version of me
It makes more sense, for a serial killer to give
me his two cents on how he'd serial kill me.
Before the cereal time of breakfast, I would be
the powder that resulted in grinding human
bones down for hours.
This made more sense to young me than the
darkness being as empty as it looks, because
nothing is at it look.
When I told my parents there was a monster
under my bed
They just laughed and said, "it's all in your
head".
But I didn't believe what they said
Because I'd seen the monster.
But, but, but
"Just stop!" They'd say.
Then pat me on the back to reassure me I was
safe

Because there wasn't a monster under my bed.
So I'm not afraid of the dark anymore…

I used to be afraid of being sad
When I'd sit and stare at my fan, and it's blades
that spun ad-infinitum
I was unfit, push-ups, I tried them
But it didn't help, mostly because the fitness I
was lacking was mental.
Then I got a dog.
And he'd stick his fluffy little face into my
hands whenever I felt sad.
Being sad just seemed boring after that,
So I wasn't afraid of being sad anymore…

I used to be afraid of sickness,
That's just because of covid.
Once I had finally accepted that I was a people
person
It was like life's puppeteer said
"Oh, you're a people person, well what if there's
no people?"
Luckily, our government stepped in with a
vaccine
So we wouldn't have to see
Half of our people cough themselves to death
So I'm not afraid of sickness anymore…

I used to be afraid of being alone

When my parents left me at home
And my dog was tired of cuddling
Until his bones, were crushed by me hugging
him like a teddy bear
So that I could steadily bear to see that scene in
that movie where the two main characters break
up.
Luckily, this was an easy solution
I just downloaded Snapchat
Then Instagram
Then X
Then, even though it's only for old people, I
downloaded facebook.
They say social media can be addicting
But they don't say how much it can be…
"Exciting!"
When you get the rush of adrenaline through
your hands from the ping of your phone.
You wouldn't expect a ding to change the way
that you think, but it does
When you won't leave your phone alone
So you just keep it in your hands.
"That was the plan all along
You got the phone because you had a stress
issue!!!"

…

"But you didn't have a stress issue until you got
your phone"

…

"No, trust me, I only have my phone because it
helps me calm down!
I get frowns when the rings are less frequent.
The sequence of my mind goes from bad to
worse
As I realize it's probably a lie when I say
I'm not afraid of being alone anymore."

I used to be afraid…
I used to be afr…
I used to be…
I used to…
I used…
I used the cutting knife
On my upper thigh.
I don't know why,
I wasn't trying to die,
But when you cry
Because of what some guy
You've never meet said about you online.
You went to write him back
And then just stared at the cursor and that stupid
blinking line
Wishing that instead of rewriting this post
You could be rewriting your life.
Because that ping doesn't give you the rattle it
once did.
Because your emotions flood in and you can't
sort 'em,

So your posts are slowly going post mortem
Just so that someone might care.
But your parents are at work, and your all alone.
…
I've climbed to the top of this mountain I didn't
realize I was trekking
When I realize that the only people that love me,
Exist on a screen that has to be
Charged and recharged just like me,
It's all fake just like me, no one loves me.
When I realize I'd forgotten depression was an
illness too,
"But depression can't kill you, until it wills you,
To put a gun to your head instead of admitting
your infected!"
When I realize that the dog that's supposed to
love me,
Doesn't love me, he runs from me,
When I call him he just gives me his voicemail
And says "Don't you ever call me back"
When I realize that I was only ever afraid of
being alone in the dark…
Because of you I'd be with.
When I realize that the monster I spent my entire
life running from was me the whole time.
…
I'm done rhyming
Rhyming is what happens when you follow a
cadence,

And things make sense.
Things keep repeating over and over again.
Yes, I am the monster
But every monster has it's puppeteer
And I'm done letting that control me.
I'm cutting the strings
Because I am done cutting myself
I am done with social media
I am done with entertaining my monsters.
I am done with being afraid,
So I'm not afraid anymore.

#UnFiltered

We used to hate our reflections in mirrors.
Now we hate how we look in the front camera
lens.
We used to hide behind the fog,
Now we hide behind our filters.
We post smiley face emojis
So we might feel them.
We wear our filters like our frowns,
Because we're unacceptable otherwise.

Forced into makeup by a beauty industry that
can't see beauty.
"Girls can only be pretty if they starve
themselves,
But still have big boobs and a pretty face.
Only pretty if they are white,
And don't have hair on their body.
Only pretty if they have the perfect hair,
The perfect nose,
The perfect cheekbones,
Perfect jawline,
Perfect skin.
They can only be beautiful if they have the
perfect body."
So all the other girls

Who wear their culture like a crown atop their
head,
Are forced to burn down their own kingdom
To be beautiful.

So to all the girls who may ever read this.
You are beautiful.
You
Are
Beautiful.
Now read that again,
And again,
Until you never forget it.
Because you are perfect for being yourself.
And it's time we all start living our lives,
#UNFiltered!

Poison

"Who's there?"
You got me caught in the crosshairs,
Where hairs cross over lost shares,
It pairs fair 'cause I don't dare
Stare down the barrel of the derringer
Tare-trigger weight away from blasting
A lasting blow with a spare, figures, 'till I'm left
to wilt-n-decay.
So, I'm locked in this cross glare
Like I'm lost in the Loch Ness
Forced to watch as the cost of this hot mess
Turns me into a monster.

Maybe Hamlet wasn't the best way to start this
poem
If I wanted to be hammin' it up by the second
stanza.
But I stand a little taller knowin' that
When I fall harder than I ever have before,
And my life stalls like the corner of a corridor
Where my soul is sold by training my core for
more,
Because I found that girl who seems to make the
pain go away.
Couldn't stand to abandon a banned relationship,

So that's how I sank the ship:
It split like an unmanned titanic.
I panicked, forcing myself to be her coy sin, the
kind that couldn't be born in her world.
Turned myself into a poison that burned the both
of us,
Because life can't fuse themselves with death
When the god's don't approve.
Plus, she had her own issues.
Her own scars across her thigh lines,
Her own fights with her mother for not letting
her SNAP like her mind desired,
Her own lungs dyed with her own kind of
Carbon Monoxide.
And as much as I tried to love her so much that
she learned to love herself,
She kept tearing me out of her heart,
And ripping the inside of mine apart as she tried
to escape.
Even when the rhymes in poetry and the words
in English stay the same…
English, unlike poetry, always has it's end.
And when the language ends, but the poem
keeps going,
The poem always ends up being about the
language it lost.
The things it lost
Lost
Lost

Lost
Lost,
And keeps losing.

And I can write all I want about how I like my
romance,
But really… mine all end up finished like
Rasputin.
Poisoned.
Rooted in a mutiny against the mirror,
Fears of mothers when bothered,
Harbored 'till she's puking, can't eat and she's
starving,
Carving her artwork into her forearm,
Before she sighs and tries the cyanide.
Goes for the O.D. when she won't see that she
can be okay
She feels the need to be leaving
Herself like Roe V. Wade,
Rolling in her grave.
But the way that I couldn't help,
Made it feel like murder, when she was
Hurting herself on the phone, it hits
Like Polonius with his foil, rips
Through your skin with a poisoned tip.
You'll never foil it,
Boil 'till you're royally toilin' mends
Your hems locked, like Hamlet, in hemlock.

Tryna be the best version of myself as I poison this
Life that she once lived.
That life that's stinted, I now know,
I wasn't prepared to have stained it.
'Cause Erros can not compare to the
Agony of Agatha Christie.
Leaving me crystallized as the brisk-told lies
Building this list of lives that I feel like I took.
And even as I look into the crystal ball,
And my life shoots before my eyes like a missile launched,
Not even the magic shtick of that mystic spawn
Could see we weren't Quantum Physics,
We were dark matter…
But at least we mattered enough to be the kind of romance we all want,
The "show me the real you and I'll show you the real me" kind of want to be love.
The "Show me your thorns and I'll show you hands willing to bleed,
Show me we're poison, and I'll show myself ready to drink,
Killing to be each other's shrinks,
Willing to sink into who we are, what we can be, what we can see,
And all the ways I can help you through any little thing that you may need."
Kind of "maybe that was love" kind of love.

Because it's not toxic that two broken people
don't know how to show their love.
They don't know who to be,
What to say,
Or how to feel that way about someone else.
And so, if you're still alive,
And you read this poem I wrote,
I hope you know that I am so sorry for not
knowing what to be for you.
But as the wind blows she goes like romeo,
I'm left to be the Juliet
Who I guess might try to find the nightshade
under the nightstand,
But can't stand to lose myself like I watched her
do.
The self harm
Put my heart in a car hardly better than war,
Horrified as it fills with Carbon monoxide.
Taking their last breath, the people inside die.
She died. She died. She died. She died. She died.
And so I searched for her obituary
"Oh bitch you scared me!"
Because I can't Bear that I lost you.
Literally lost you.
My face drained, it's gaunt and,
My heart becomes haunted,
'Cause haunted things are just the places people
die in.
And…

I may have been poison, but at least I made you fucking feel something.
Then again, who wants to feel anything in a world so cold.
As the told story goes, it folds, in the end when…
Every poison is its own antidote.

Solitary Confinement

I've spent half of my life in solitary confinement
Alone in a room with a straitjacket
Trying as hard as I can to go so crazy
That I seem normal enough to want to leave.

Cleansed, Again

I feel like,
For the last half of my life,
I have been hospitalized.
Trapped in an asylum
In a white walled room designed
For keeping solitary people confined.
Staring at the white walls while my sanity's still
mine.
I'm locked away,
Starting from the same time
Mental Illness was placed on the
"Fear this or die" map.
I mean look into my eyes,
Can't you see that I might
Snap?
Might sneak into your house in the middle of the
night,
Murder your family, crack your spine.
I tried so hard to be normal
Until I was silenced by The Silence of the
Lambs,
And slammed down by Psycho,
Before I got hexed, maimed wrong, and mass
cursed
By the Texas Chainsaw Massacre.

And that mask, it hurt but taking it off hurt
worse
Because when people really saw that part of me.
They were afraid of me. They were afraid of me.
They were afraid of me. They were afraid of me.
They were afraid of me. They were afraid of me.
They were afraid of me. They were afraid of me.
They were afraid of me. They were afraid of me.
They were afraid of me. They were afraid of me.
They were afraid of me. They were afraid of me.
They were afraid of me. They were afraid of me.
They were afraid of me. They were afraid of me.
They were afraid of me. They were afraid of me.
They were afraid of me. They were afraid of me.
They were afraid of me. They were afraid of me.
They were afraid of me. They were afraid of me.
They were afraid of me. They were afraid of me.
They were afraid of me. They were afraid of me.
They were afraid of me. They were afraid of me.
They were afraid of me. They were afraid of me.
They were afraid of me. They were afraid of me.
They were afraid of me. They were afraid of me.
They were afraid of me. They were afraid of me.
They were afraid of me. They were afraid of me.
They were afraid of me. They were afraid of me.
They were afraid of me. They were afraid of me.
They were afraid of the same part of me that I
feared even more.

And this explosive fear and hate is the reason we
can See Four
Mentally Ill teens sink to the seafloor.
We're sheep who silently speak in lion's roars
As we weep 'cause we need more
People to listen when we ask for help.
But instead we're cast to hell, screaming:
What the hell! What the hell! What the hell!
What the hell! What the hell! What the Hell!
What the hell! What the hell! What the hell!
What the hell! What the hell! What the Hell!
What the hell! What the hell! What the hell!
What the hell! What the hell! What the Hell!
What the hell! What the hell! What the hell!
What the hell! What the hell! What the Hell!
What the hell! What the hell! What the hell!
What the hell! What the hell! What the Hell!
What the hell! What the hell! What the hell!
What the hell! What the hell! What the Hell!
What the hell! What the hell! What the hell!
What the hell! What the hell! What the Hell!
What the hell! What the hell! What the hell!
What the hell! What the hell! What the Hell!
What the hell did you lock me away for?
I feel like society trying to make me
The main character in a Sarah Kane story.
Trying to store me down below and cleanse me
of my identity.

I'm storming against the seas of those who don't
see me for me,
Trying to forge my way through streams of those
who think
That I am the weakest of the human species.
That I am
Scary,
Threatening,
And incurable
Because of my curable disease.
And everyone's pleased to use
The news media to prove
That those who have suffered more,
Deserve to have their necks jammed in a noose.
That if you are mentally ill,
You have to pop these pills
To kill every part of who you are,
To paint white over your arts, and distill your
skills.
They'll stab through your soul like a pelican bill;
Gelatin brains to replace what once filled the
space behind your face.
So at Four Forty-Eight you'll write on a piece of
paper.
I swear to god,
I'm not crazy! I'm not crazy! I'm not crazy! I'm
not crazy! I'm not crazy! I'm not crazy!
I'm not crazy! I'm not crazy! I'm not crazy! I'm
not crazy! I'm not crazy! I'm not crazy!

I'm not crazy! I'm not crazy! I'm not crazy! I'm
not crazy! I'm not crazy! I'm not crazy!
I'm not crazy! I'm not crazy! I'm not crazy! I'm
not crazy! I'm not crazy! I'm not crazy!
I'm not crazy! I'm not crazy! I'm not crazy! I'm
not crazy! I'm not crazy! I'm not crazy!
I'm not crazy! I'm not crazy! I'm not crazy! I'm
not crazy! I'm not crazy! I'm not crazy!
I'm not crazy! I'm not crazy! I'm not crazy! I'm
not crazy! I'm not crazy! I'm not crazy!
I'm not crazy! I'm not crazy! I'm not crazy! I'm
not crazy! I'm not crazy! I'm not crazy!
I'm not crazy but I feel like I'm losing it more
everyday.
And I feel like I'm free-falling into an abyss of
"kane me 'till I love the world no more".
Like these colonizing ant colonies can't stop
their raging wars
Against the larger hordes
Of their own people.
To cleanse the world of those who don't
conform.
It's like they like to watch their own as they fall
on their rotting skin.
As the leaders install their policies of
lobotomies…
"NO!
It's not a lobotomy
Because that's not what we call it, see?"

- Says the medical industry
As they push their unproven ways to treat
These problems that we
Could solve if we sat down for three seconds
and listened to all of our hurting people when
they screamed.
But no, this is the end
For anyone who's different.
And as the mentally ill are pieces of minced
meat of what they used to be
The greater world is pleased that we can be…
Cleansed again. Cleansed again. Cleansed again.
Cleansed again. Cleansed again. Cleansed again.
Cleansed again. Cleansed again. Cleansed again.
Cleansed again. Cleansed again. Cleansed again.
Cleansed again. Cleansed again. Cleansed again.
Cleansed again. Cleansed again. Cleansed again.
Cleansed again. Cleansed again. Cleansed again.
Cleansed again. Cleansed again. Cleansed again.
Cleansed again. Cleansed again. Cleansed again.
Cleansed again. Cleansed again. Cleansed again.
Cleansed again. Cleansed again. Cleansed again.
Cleansed again. Cleansed again. Cleansed again.
Cleansed again. Cleansed again. Cleansed again.
Cleansed again. Cleansed again. Cleansed again.
Cleansed again. Cleansed again. Cleansed again.
Cleansed again. Cleansed again. Cleansed again.
And no one
Even

Notices

As we pen our protest in poetry
To try to cope with this dystopian loss of hope.
But our words sink on the sea like toy boats in a
storm,
On these tongue twisting times that know we
can't stay afloat much longer.
But I swear on all of the Sarah Kane stories,
And Ayn Rand Anthems!
I swear on every stanza that stands to represent
who we are!
And I swear on all that I am,
All I will be,
And all I have been!
We will NEVER be
CLEANSED
AGAIN!

Atlas

Atlas:
The man who held the world on his shoulders;
Wrapped in the wrath of a zealous Zeus,
He was forced to hold the whole of the world on
the flat of his aching back.
And every day he held it, the world grew
heavier.

If you could smell the sweat pouring from the
Titan's face
And you could tell the wet sores across his body
were from where he bled,
As the earth pushed him further in the spot
where he stayed.
What would you tell him?

If you could feel the muscles across his body
As they writhed around the world so as not to
disturb it.
If you could feel how much it hurt him.
If you could taste the Titan's determination
Through your own hatred.
Taste how he bore so much weight, and never
even made a sound.

If you could hear the utter silence of the Titan as
he struggled
How dare you suggest he might shrug.

If you saw Atlas
As he held the world upon his shoulders.
As his body collapsed from the inside.
If you saw how hard he tried to keep the world
aloft.
How he destroyed himself.
If you saw the blood running down his body,
If you saw the bruises on his back,
If you saw how the gods wiped away his tears,
Because no man like that should ever cry.
If you saw as Zeus added more weight.
As Hesperis ripped his heart from his crumbling
chest
So the god's could call him heartless.
If you saw Atlas punished for the actions of
those like him,
And you saw his living corpse enduring his
punishment.
If you saw Atlas, in his dying moments
When the world became too much.
When he could no longer be the Titan who bears
all the weight so quietly.
If you saw him crush himself to death.
If you saw the way he died under the weight of
that life he never chose.

What would you tell him?

He was weak for trembling under the world's
weight?
He was pathetic for bleeding from his cuts?
He was not a real man because he could not hold
that world up forever?
Or
He was Evil for never crying?
He was awful for his heartlessness?
He was unlovable because of the weight the
world pressed into his back?

Atlas was unacceptable
Because he existed.

Bears

I always thought I was a good person.
Or at least I always tried to be a good person.
I will always help if someone hurts themselves,
Or be there for my short friends who can't reach
their top shelves.
And I used to do this because I believed in God
and Santa Claus.
But I learned as I got older that Santa Claus and
his elves were just my parents,
And that the great stories of God and his choice
of burning in hell, just…
Wasn't for me.
And even after that I tried to do nice things.
I would walk old ladies across the street,
And donate all of my money to Charity so
people could eat,
And I still do those things, those nice things.
But I don't think that I'm a good person
anymore,
Because of how many horrible things were done
by people who look like me.

"Would you rather be lost in the woods with a
Man or a Bear?

Bear.
Because at least they'll believe me when I say it
attacked me.
I would rather be with the bear,
Because the Bear wouldn't keep his intentions
hidden.
The Bear wouldn't stare through my clothes.
The Bear wouldn't go absolutely livid
If I told him I would've picked the man.
…
The Bear wouldn't go back to other bears and
brag
That he snagged and ragdolled me in my dead
body."

The first time I really realized I was a real guy
Was when I started to see how girls would writh
uncomfortably around me.
Because they were scared that I would leave
them to be one of the one in three statistics.
And it's sick and sadistic that in our society,
It's one in three women who are sexually
assaulted.
So that the women become she-shell shells of
who they want to be.
Then we're all left wondering: well if this
happens to a third of our girls

What's the number of men who are burning their
worlds?
The number of men who are yearning for the
types of love that must be forced.
The number of men who prey on those who pray
for better lives every night and through their
days?
And why is society able to look them in the face
While they look away from learning from their
mistakes?
Why is our best response to rape to victim
blame?
Why is our best treatment is to make them
victims again,
And again,
And again,
And shame them for ever being victims in the
first place?

"Would you rather be lost in the woods with a
Man or a Bear?
Would you rather be lost with a
Horrifying,
Violent,
And untamed beast,
Or a Bear?
You would rather the Bear.
Bears never commit genocide,

Bears never enslaved each other
Bears never showed the world their dark side,
Their stark side,
Their criminally insane insides:
The villainy hiding in the minds of men.
A bear might kill you but they wouldn't enjoy
it."

The next time I realized I was a guy was when I
found on this website
That men are four times more likely to commit
suicide.
And that one in five guys have been sexually
assaulted in their lifetimes
But only one in every twenty five is fine with
coming to the light and speaking up about it.
Yeah, we tout ourselves at totally fine, and say
it's alright
'Cause we were taught to pop pills
'Till we shrivel inside.
We're taught that men don't cry.
We hold all we feel right behind our eyes
And even if we go blind, or insane, you just
keep hanging in there.
Hang on your own rope, and stick to the old
trope
That when the sadness takes over,

You turn your pain into rage to break through all
of the madness and angst.
Because a real man slaughters and rapes,
A real man beats his daughters and his son's fill
his shoes,
Shoots bullets through roofs.
Roofies a real girl's drink.
Real men don't really think.
And when life just seems like it's not worth
living
Then a real man grows a Bear sized pair of balls
He pulls a gun and blasts his brains across the
wall.
And deep down, these real men wait for the day
That Rand was right, and they can shrug the
weight,
Of always having to be worse than a Bear on
cocaine,
Off of their shoulders.
So that at last
They don't have to be trapped like Atlas.

"Would you rather be lost in the woods with a
Man or a Bear?
You KNOW you would prefer the Bear.
You have to prefer the Bear.
Can't you see how the man's society always
silences screams?

How could you ever prefer the man if you see
men for what they truly are?"

Someone once told me I couldn't advocate for
men's mental health
Then turn around and claim that I'm feminist
against rape.
As if the two aren't the same problem dressed in
differently stressed ways.
The same world that turns the word "victim" to a
slur,
Is the same world that carves our brave men into
caves.
Starves their caveman hearts until they're empty
on the inside
And sharpens their dark edges to be sharp
enough to sharp shoot themselves with.
But people wonder why men can't bear that
women prefer the bear
When we're told by the world that this is the
face we're supposed to wear.
Then told that we are the problem instead of the
world who made us wear the face.

The problem holding our men down
And putting us into the ground, round after
round.

The same idea that pushed us to become assault
guns
The reason millions of men are weapons of
destruction
Self-destructing nuclear warheads,
Hot headed balls of lead
Better Found On Road Dead,
Is the same reason women's screams are gagged
under hands
And the world can't understand why no one can
breathe
'Cause women are being choked out, and men
are choking themselves with their own tears.

The reason why women say prayers.
Why they fear walking at night whenever a man
is near.
The reason why thousands of women across the
nation
Flounder on the internet and yell in
conversations.
The reason they all agree they want the bear:
Men are thousands of generations of taking
poundings and hatred
They are powder kegs of unfelt despair.
So you tell me how is it fair that you blame men
When society failed them too?
But instead of working it through,
Together, to gather the root of the issue.

Men scream at women for being scared of the
people the men were made to be.
While women call men toxic
For being boxed in
By the very same toxins
That locked this ridiculous world in as ours.
And instead of having taught kids
How to be good people
Who feel their emotions,
And don't bottle it in.
Instead of people trying to fight against higher
society,
Make it okay for guys to go cry,
Admit they were raped,
And ask for help if they need it.
Let women actually speak when they say they
were taken,
And wonder "what if we don't victim blame
them"?
We ask about companions in the woods.
I just don't think the world understands what's at
stake,
When we aren't helping to undertake our
problems,
Because we're arguing on tiktok instead of
trying to solve them.

"Would you rather be lost in the woods with a Man or a Bear?"

If I was lost in the woods…
I would stay lost in the woods.

Vacuum Lady

They say, in a vacuum, no one can hear you
scream.
Personally, I've never been in one,
'Cause Dyson doesn't make them in my size.
But, every day, I see people screaming from
inside them.
Trapped like a penny on a Bell Jar.
They bang against the glass wall holding them
in,
And apparently no one hears them.
That sucks, right?

Those poor vacuum ladies
Living their vacuum lives
Of vacuuming and doing chores
…
What's the difference between
Ironman
And
Ironwoman?
One is a superhero,
And the other is a command.
HAHAHAHAHAHAHAHAHAHAHAHAHAHAH
AHAHAHAHAHAHAHAHAHAHAHAHAHAHH
AHAHAHAHAHAHAHHAAH!

No, but seriously,
Any woman reading this poetry book
Should stop immediately.
Because otherwise they just might get smart
enough to realize
How ridiculous it is to be a vacuum lady.
They have to stick to their vacuums,
And make these chores their identity.
Join the cult of domesticity, and just be
Vacuum ladies.

They say, in a vacuum, no one can hear you
scream.
But even if they could.
It doesn't matter.
Because vacuum ladies shouldn't be screaming
anyway.
They should stay silent, because look at all they
have in their vacuums.
The right to work,
For
Less
Money.
And the right to speak up,
Unless
They
Have
Something
To

Say.

Because a vacuum lady is a woman devoid of
matter.
A woman without matter,
Without importance,
Without a voice,
Without MATTERING!
Contained in a glass box, void of anything,
And so low in pressure that any matter-ing that
seeps inside
Can make no difference.
But, then, the people that built these boxes
Will speak to the vacuum ladies trapped inside.
They will tell them they can break the glass
ceiling of the box,
To set the vacuum ladies free.
And the ladies in the vacuum choose these
people as their leaders.
The "leaders" who turn around and say the same
thing four years later
As they slowly drain the life of the vacuum
ladies.
It's all of those women who sell other women
into sex slavery,
The women who trap women in a #Filtered
version of themselves because otherwise they
will never be acceptable,
And the women who run for office,

Build their bridge to the white house on votes
from other women.
Then make sure that they make no change
So they can stay in power.
The men who rape women,
And tell them to keep their mouths shut.
The men who don't pay women enough to live
outside of their vacuums.
It's the men who run for office on the basic idea
of taking the right to ideas away from women.
…
What's the difference between
A
Woman
And
A
Victim?
Nothing.
Because the two have become so similar no one
can even tell the difference anymore.

They say, in a vacuum, no one can hear you
scream.
They're wrong.
In this vacuum,
Everyone
Hears
You
Scream.

Shots; The Intervention

My grandmother used to be a nurse
And part of that medical curse
Is knowing how to treat the cuts and burns that
hurt the worst.
She learned how to hide the slash lines behind
Hydrogen Peroxide.
Because alcohol leaves any injury sterilized.
So, as a kid, when she would gash the side of her
knee
She would kneel herself beside the corner of the
street
And leave the nasty gnash cornered and beat
As she poured on her uniquely secret remedy
Then two or three minutes later she would be
Totally normal and back to playing games and
smiling.
So for any nick-nack nick on the skin or nack on
the back
She always had a cure.

But, unlike, the wounds of her youth,
They moved to the inside as she grew
And even as the cuts left her skin and stained her
brain.

Her only way to mend her pain, was to burn it
away, and leave herself cleansed
So when she lost her husband, the guide to her
world.
Her Atlas, her map
That loss was not a gash but a gap
Between every heartbeat.
And that gap increased
Every time she treats her tears and mournings
With another sting of the scald of the alcohol.
…
When she lost her niece
And the tears hurt worse than her old scrapes on
the knee
Because she couldn't believe these kinds of
things really happen
To people who believe in goodness.
She pushed her emotions back again
With the soothing cleanliness of alcohol burning
her tears back into her brain.
Because she always had a cure.

The problem with treating every problem with
alcohol
Is that it can only temporarily clean the wound.
It makes everything seem better for the moment
But stops you from healing.
So watching my grandmother burn away her
feelings

Watching her peel decayed layers of her skin
when she burns them away
And not being able to say a damn thing
Because that's the way she learned to deal with
cuts and kinks in the road.
It hurts.
I want to intervene, but she thinks that tears
Make her tears and cuts seem unclean.
And she's drowning in her fear of drowning.
She…
Spends all of her time three sheets to the wind
And spends everything she has to burn those
feelings again,
Shooting her thoughts with shots lined across the
bar
And into my heart
Because she refuses to admit she hurts.
She refuses to admit that she doesn't have a
cure.
And not having a cure should be okay…
But my Grandmother used to be a nurse
And part of that medical curse
Is always having to treat the cuts and burns that
hurt the worst.
She learned to always hide behind her hydrogen
peroxide
Because she'll be totally fine if she flies the "I'm
not okay" to the bottom side of a bottle of wine.

If she puts all of it down the pipe every single
night
She will be totally alright.
But she's not
She's not alright
And more alcohol is not going to fix that.

Freely *Censored* Speaking

This Poem Has Been Censored by the United States Federal Government
Luckily it has been Replaced with the below message

"The USFG Censors poems such as this for YOUR protection; Because silence hurts, but thoughts can kill."

"You're welcome American citizens!"

Tongue Twisters

I used to love tongue twisters.
Totally titillating tongue tied,
Try to say it five times fast,
It's a tongue twisting blast
When you look past the fact that the words don't
pack a pact, or a meaning
They just let you relax and repeat words others
spat.
But, in the end, that's the trap.

So Sally seems to sell seashells by the seashore
Well, what of the hell the tell-tale she-shells,
endured?
When Sally sold the sorry, sucker, small girls by
the seashore?
Yes, Sally sold six slues of the silly seeming,
solely screaming girls
To short shaven, bald, cravin', sully satin men,
who's words run the world.
And sure, this may seem like an awful thing,
selling sex slaves by the sea shore
But the truth is no one's scared, or cares until it
may seem mainstream,
But even these things easily sweep under rugs
and out of streams.

So they put back to sleep, Sally's poor girl's and
their screams
Because they already sold reality.

Peter Piper picked a peck of pipes and joined a
pro-Palestinian protest last night
To support the rights of a terribly tyrannical
terrorist government
And their plight to fight those not a far cry from
a part time apartheid.
Stopped a Jewish boy as he was leaving class, he
was crying.
They called him a Zionist for trying his highest
to make it to mass again.
But he was pushed out of the way by the
fake-enraged minute made renegades
Properly paid to make it okay to hate anyone
that doesn't see the world "your" way.
Exterminate the innocent Israelis because you
were told to hate them!
Persecute the peaceful Palestinians and partake
in their displacement
Because they're not from your nation.
Scream in the faces of the needy and beam as
they revel on leveled homes and live in their
lustrous rubble.
As the millionaires make their millions of bucks
On the millions in trucks leaving the dust that
was once people's... everything.

These tongue twisted wars always have a
winner, and it's never the people.
No humans can win in war.
But the tongue twisting terrorization
Of ostracizing others as rotten to the core,
For not conforming to laws they'd never
adorned,
And the half hearted hatred of people in wars
Simply because you misunderstood what they
stand for
…
It has to stop.

It's all of those terrible,
Tear a hole in the veritable vertebrae of validity,
Tally's taking brains for stupidity,
Making vast valleys in rallies.
Fastly forgetting the past and happily wearing
their caste.
And as you lose your violets and roses
They water down violence with hoses
And we know this, but down wanna blow it
Out of proportion.
'Cause who needs abortions
When we the people have the right to be born in
A world torn by the torrent of horrible whores
Tryna open the doors of their mouths and speak
free
Like they don't know, or can't see that it's 1984.

And your big siblings have more spies,
In the streets and through the floor
Than you have weeks
To count how weak you are with chloroform
From the coroner pressed up against your cheek.
Go back to the little diddles:
The totally not hoax right to vote,
To cast your casting call for
Tom Riddle or the Devil with his fiddle
And forget about the people in the middle!
Meanwhile, the mean-vile notorious Big Brother
watches
The must be stopped caucus concoct a gun
cocked conscious
And stop, with rounds and pound with rocks,
any punk kids making a raucous.
Shoot those that you fear clear through the ear
Because we can guarantee your freedom of
speech,
But don't ever think you're free after you speak
On social m-Idi. A. (media)
Because if you speak free but you disagree
You have the right to watch your words burn at
Four hundred and fifty one degrees.
Watch as we churn these books about identity
And send them Four Hundred leagues into the
sea.
Or put them Fifty times higher in the sky than
anyone can even see,

Because we'll always have Won, we're too
Far-in-height
To be caught or called out on our appalling
appeal.
Even when it almost feels, like
You'll be totally fine
As long as you pray to the undead gods who
aren't in the sky.
"Surrender yourself
And don't ask us why.
But the walls have our eyes
Searching for what's left as right; fully mine".
But an eye for an eye, and the world goes blind
Then we can't find what's left as bonafide
through what they tried to hide
In these brain teasing, tongue twisting party trick
rhymes.
Perfectly designed to keep the thinking one's
quiet,
Because you can't speak up, when your twisted
tongue is tied.

"Our whole lives we've been looking for
monsters.
We check under beds,
And we check inside ourselves.
But we never found them.
We keep getting told these stories of monsters
So that we'll look for them,

Instead of finding them in the one's telling us the stories."

- Coby Jones, 2024. Tongue Twisted.

Roses are Red...

Roses are red
And violets are blue
This entire poems a trope
And the idea's overused
Because really…

Some states are red
And others are blue
And each of them do
Exactly what they're supposed to, when…

Your kids bleed red
Because others were blue
And walked into school
With a gun to shoot.
They painted their rage through a barrel
And barreled their bullets through bullies.
Spraying their hate across the faces of
classmates'
Bloodstains where he led lead through throats.
The senate's staring at your children, pained and
dead,
After he painted the world like the cemetery in
his head.
And this kind of violence blue our minds inside
of rhymes

You wrote, recite and rise, but once they rose,
they are not red.

So the masses sway across the hallways with
mass graves
Dug by crass raves and rants, in political mask
games
And those with the brass stance where they stay
They say to only see it "their way"
They'd drown, or fight a spouse
So that no one sins with their mouth
Because the - White - House always wins.

Our present tense press sets the precedence
For our presidents to never make a difference
Since kids walk through schools with clenched
fists
And sophist politicians act "so pissed" when
they rant
And return to their fairyland
Funded by some companies that run guns for
fun.
And the monochromatic monarchy will stand
In front of their millions of stans, with billions
of plans
That just have to wait, because to take action is
to make change.
I know it stings, but it's all ran by hate.

And we want to feel a real fairyland, but at this
rate
Our faerie queens are trapped in a stalemate.
And our children stay staked against a stale fate
Where the color that they bleed is the color of
their state
Because, in the end, it's all a state of mind
And, apparently, it has to stay that way, no
matter how many of us die.
For them to yell from heaven, we are cast into
the kind of hell
Where bullets melt into class bells.

So roses are red
And violets are blue
Your kids are dead
And their bodies used
As fuel for a foule parliament's bowels.
These flowers are delicate in poems, and words
But when the delicacy of our youth is hurt
We can scream 'till it burns, but we're never
heard
Until we break from the herd, and realize…

Roses aren't so red
And violets aren't so blue
Society is stuck running in a kind of unsweet
honey
And, well, so are me and you.

Elevator Capacity

Elevator Capacity:
3 people.
If too many people are trying to go up on the
elevator with you.
You will all go down.

Elevator Capacity:
2 people.
No bags.
If you board with too much baggage.
You will never leave your floor.

Elevator Capacity:
You
Just you.
No baggage.
No extra weight.
To go up, you have to just be you,
With nothing to hide behind.

Espresso Boy

Espresso Boy:
Bland and flavorless until roasted.
But not burnt, because coffee doesn't go with
toast.

Espresso boy:
Grinding himself down to become art.
Feeling trapped in a vacuum chamber,
With the weight of nine worlds on his back
Like he's Atlas but nine times over.
The weight of the nine bars his grandmother
drank at last night
One Hundred and Thirty
"P.S.I am so sorry things didn't work out with
us"
Bearing down on him.
Until the ground down espresso boy can't take
it.
Lets the pressure pass through him.
Turns it into something else.
Something beautiful,
Something Uninspired.

Espresso Boy:
You can taste, on your twisted tongue,

His roots, his home, his childhood,
The world he came from,
How he was roasted,
And his floral rose-like undertones.
The art he became is unfiltered, and freely
uncensored,
Not afraid to say what is happening.

Espresso Boy:
Becomes the kind of art that created him.

www.ingramcontent.com/pod-product-compliance
Lightning Source LLC
La Vergne TN
LVHW011044200726
843509LV00011B/1351